Born Liquid

To Zygmunt, to whom I owe everything.
To Aleksandra, Lydia, Anna,
Irena, Maurice and Mark:

I am so grateful that life made our paths cross.

THOMAS LEONCINI

Zygmunt Bauman
Thomas Leoncini

Born Liquid

Transformations in the Third Millennium

Passages from the Italian
translated by Lucinda Byatt

polity

First published in Italian as *Nati liquidi. Trasformazioni nel terzo millennio*
© Sperling & Kupfer Editori S.p.A, 2017

This English edition © Polity Press, 2019

The right of Lucinda Byatt to be identified as translator of the Italian passages in this work has been asserted in accordance with Section 77 of the Copyright, Designs and Patents Act 1988.

Polity Press
65 Bridge Street
Cambridge CB2 1UR, UK

Polity Press
101 Station Landing
Suite 300
Medford, MA 02155, USA

ISBN-13: 978-1-5095-3067-0
ISBN-13: 978-1-5095-3068-7 (pb)

A catalogue record for this book is available from the British Library.

Library of Congress Cataloging-in-Publication Data
Names: Bauman, Zygmunt, 1925-2017, author. | Leoncini, Thomas, 1985- author.
Title: Born liquid : transformations in the third millennium / Zygmunt
Bauman, Thomas Leoncini.
Other titles: Nati liquidi. English
Description: Cambridge, UK ; Medford, MA : Polity Press, [2018] | Includes
bibliographical references and index.
Identifiers: LCCN 2018012971 (print) | LCCN 2018029270 (ebook) | ISBN
9781509530700 (Epub) | ISBN 9781509530670 (hardback) | ISBN 9781509530687
(pbk.)
Subjects: LCSH: Postmodernism--Social aspects. | Social change--Philosophy. |
Civilization, Modern--21st century. | Social history--21st century.
Classification: LCC HM449 (ebook) | LCC HM449 .B39513 2018 (print) | DDC
909.83--dc23
LC record available at https://lccn.loc.gov/2018012971

Typeset in 12.5 on 15pt Adobe Garamond by
Servis Filmsetting Ltd, Stockport, Cheshire

Printed and bound in Great Britain by Clays Ltd, Popson Street,
Bungay, Elcograf S.p.A.

For further information on Polity, visit our website: politybooks.com

On 21 February 2017, an international seminar held at the Kolegium Artes Liberales of the University of Warsaw, Poland, was held to celebrate Zygmunt Bauman's theory of liquid modernity. I was asked to talk about my husband's last works and I began by describing the joint project with a young man to write about the younger generations, those who are *Born Liquid*. I told the audience about how they corresponded and how the young man was committed to finishing the book after Zygmunt's departure into 'liquid eternity'. The lecture hall was packed to overflowing, and an even wider audience was listening online, linked from various parts of the world. There was enormous interest. I believe there could not be a better augury for the long voyage undertaken by this little book.

ALEKSANDRA KANIA BAUMAN

With the demise of my individual body, bodily existence will not really end. It will continue, much as it started before the appearance of my body and before the beginning of my own thinking, before my 'entering the world'. It will continue in the form of the bodily presence of other people.

ZYGMUNT BAUMAN, *Mortality,
Immortality and other Life Strategies**

* Zygmunt Bauman, *Mortality, Immortality and other Life Strategies*, Cambridge: Polity, 1992, p. 18.

Contents

I

Skin-deep transformations

Tattoos, plastic surgery, hipsters

Thomas Leoncini:

Young people are a snapshot of the changing times. It is impossible not to love them and hate them simultaneously. They are what we love most about our 'past', but also what we instinctively detest, because it didn't last forever; it was fluid, liquid. Today, when we analyse what being young means, we are victims of a failed cultural relativism – one that is impossible to put into practice efficiently, simply because it doesn't exist outside ourselves, an 'us' that looks on at the doorway of the ego. As we look at the young, we look with the gaze of liquefied persons who have inevitably altered their own boundaries: we are the product of whatever life's circumstances have made us. The product of that *us* that today is no longer part of our present and can therefore do nothing except see itself in other people's faces. If it's true that the mind travels using cultural schemas created by our brains in order to

3

respond rapidly to any situational event (this is what cognitive psychology says), it is equally true that often our struggle to tolerate the young is also motivated by the regret that we didn't make the best of, understand or fully observe our earlier life before we unconsciously found ourselves in the current one.

So, when we look at a young boy, perhaps of school-leaving age or thereabouts, we no longer see him using the frame of mind that we had when we were his age, but rather using our completely liquefied schemas – ones that belong to different people, people who are now *others* compared to what we were then.

Put in even simpler terms: to us, the traits shown by the young, so replete with the present, are unrecognizable, whether as the individual offspring of our desire for self-affirmation, or in terms of aesthetic fashion, that reality which is often undervalued but essential because it pervades and invades our gaze.

'Appearance is for me that which lives and is effective', wrote Nietzsche,[1] and, in this, the

---

[1] Friedrich Nietzsche, *The Gay Science*, Leipzig: E. W. Fritzsch, 1887, p. 102.

young represent the mass change par excellence of styles and interests linked to the present, which anthropologists have realized is the most important element of their borderline science, by definition incomplete and unrealized in its fragmented entirety, to the extent that it transforms anthropology from biological and palaeoanthropological physics into cultural and social anthropology. And the young are the most representative examples of what we will become, today and tomorrow. Even Aristotle defined mankind as incomplete.

But the desire for completion (while undoubtedly vain and illusory) has been present since the dawn of civilization. So what could be better than our body as the stage on which to enact a presentation of self? The aesthetic sense, it should be remembered, is partly subjective and objective, but, above all, also cultural and collective.

We often talk about the aesthetic phenomenon as the most representative fashion of the modern age, but fashions are anthropopoietic[2] – that is to say, they form part of the knowing construction

---

[2] A term introduced and circulated in Italy by the anthropologist Francesco Remotti.

of *being* human. From the earliest times, humans have refused to leave their bodies as they are and they have always been determined to alter them, based, to varying degree, on the dominant culture. Even washing ourselves every morning is nothing more than a representation of the relationship humans have with their bodies, the need to change it *vis-à-vis* the natural 'run of things': in this respect, the English anthropologist Mary Douglas stated that hygiene is not just a question of scientific progress.

Aesthetic fashions, like cultural ones, are dynamic, and therefore it is particularly useful to start from the clash, the spark, the explosion that results in the genesis of cultural reformulation, fanned by the embrace (a lethal one for models of the past) between one's own models and mass models. The latter have invaded the adult world through imitation, contagion or natural ageing.

A representative example of one of the most current fashions is tattoos, which are widely present in all age groups, from the very young to the young, and even adults.

Three out of ten Americans have tattoos, and most do not stop at the first. These are some of the findings of a recent survey by The Harris Poll, according to which, tattoos are seen as virtually indispensable by young Americans: almost half of Millennials (47%) and over a third of Generation Xers (36%) have at least one. By Millennials, I mean the famous generation Y, born between 1980 and 2000 – the genesis of the current 'born liquid' generation – while Gen Xers are those who were born between roughly the mid-sixties and the late seventies or early eighties.

On the other hand, only 13% of Baby Boomers (those born between 1946 and 1964) have a tattoo. Of course, the boundaries between these definitions have never been static, resembling something blurred or liquid, to keep to the same theme. Given their high percentages, Millennials and Gen Xers will obviously extend the trend considerably, and therefore, in a few years' time, the data for 50-, 60-, 70- and 80-year-olds with tattoos will be completely reversed. Another interesting fact to emerge from the survey is that place of residence has no influence at all on whether Americans consider it fashionable to have a tattoo. Whether you're a country- or a city-dweller, there are no significant – or even any particularly representative – differences. The same applies to political orientation:

Republicans 27%, Democrats 29%, independents 28%.

For Italy, the latest data come from the national Health Institute (Istituto Superiore di Sanità): 13 out of every 100 Italians have tattoos. With a calculator to hand, that means there are some 7 million tattooed Italians. The data also reveal that more women have tattoos than men (13.8% of the women interviewed, compared to 11.7% of men). The average age at which people get their first tattoo is 25, but the highest percentage of people with tattoos is in the 35- to 45-year-old age bracket (29.9%). Approximately 1.5 million people with tattoos are aged between 25 and 34 years old, with a percentage of 7.7% for under 18-year-olds. The vast majority are pleased with their tattoos (92.2%), but quite a high percentage – as many as 17.2% – would like to have them removed; and, of these, 4.3% have already done so. The men prefer a tattoo on their arms, shoulders and legs; the women, above all, on their back, feet and ankles. One tattooed person out of four (25.1%) lives in northern Italy, 30.7% are graduates, and 63.1% are in work; 76% had their tattoos applied in a specialized centre, 9.1% in a beauty salon, but a large group, 13.4%, had them done by an unlicensed practitioner. Again in

Italy, there are no relevant details regarding political loyalty – a brand to be impressed on the skin as the sign of a lifetime's adherence to an ideal. Yet doesn't everyone remember tattoos being used as a representative sign of political cohesion or creed? Today this has disappeared completely, and the political 'motive' for the tattoo has been engulfed by our liquid modernity.

Today, political motivations have been completely redesigned – perhaps it would be better to say (with greater pathos) 'restructured' – by individuality. This is because the dividing line between the public and private spheres has been eradicated at its very root. Our private issues constantly invade the public sphere, but this does not mean that our problems become other people's problems. Quite the opposite: our problems remain our own. Instead, it means that, thanks to our reducing the public sphere to a 'begging pitch', we literally destroy the space for all those topics that really belong there. The result is that politics, understood as citizens' political agency within the public debate, is now dead. The scope of action of today's 'born liquid' generation is bounded by each member's own individuality, and they frantically try to give it public notoriety by invading the public sphere and deluding themselves that a universal solution for its incompleteness can exist, and even be shared by all.

The question that comes to mind is why have tattoos become necessary for anyone who wants to conform to the aesthetics of liquid modernity?

Zygmunt Bauman:

All the new and striking copy-cat modes of manipulating the public appearances of one's body (or the 'presentation of self in everyday life', as Erving Goffman preferred to brand them), which you noted and listed above so perceptively – all of them short-lived (although, as Charles Baudelaire observed more than century and a half ago, all of them aiming to capture eternity in a fleeting moment) – have their roots in the modern, all-too-human recasting of social identity from a *given* into a *task*. It is a task that today is expected, needed and bound to be performed by its individual bearer, while deploying socially supplied patterns and raw materials in a complex operation of 'creative reproduction', which goes by the name of 'fashion'.

As Eric Hobsbawm, arguably the greatest historian of the last century, suggested, ever since the idea of 'community' started to be relegated to the margins of social thought and practice (and even earmarked for extinction, courtesy of the once highly influential sociologist Ferdinand Tönnies and the multitude of his nineteenth- and twentieth-century followers), the idea of 'identity' and the practice of 'self-identification' have erupted to fill the void which the antici- pated disappearance of the latter would create in the extant routines of social placement and classification.

Thomas Leoncini:
Community and identity are separated by a line that often seems insurmountable in our society.

Zygmunt Bauman:
The difference between community and identity is formidable. In principle, the first is obliga- tory and coercive as it determines and defines in advance the individual's social casting; the second is presumed to be 'freely chosen' and a 'do-it- yourself' job. Rather than eliminating community from the processes of social placement and its expression, such conceptual replacement aims

to reconcile the (should we say irreconcilable?) challenges of 'belonging' with the self-definition coupled with self-assertion.

The endemic, incurable inclination for conflict-generation and the complex dialectics – as well as the astonishing dynamics – of the fashion phenomenon stem from here, as do its creative capabilities and irreparable frailties; and it is this that sustains them and keeps them in action.

No one, in my view, has provided a more detailed vivisection of fashion – fashion as a product (by its nature, constantly under pressure to renew) of that dialectics of belonging and individuality – than Georg Simmel, who wrote and was published at the turn of the nineteenth and twentieth centuries, that is, during the fateful era of transition from the society of producers to that of consumers. It is a vivisection that remains extraordinarily relevant, which we still reproduce today, while being reproduced, groomed and honed by it.

Thomas Leoncini:
When you watch a football match, it's difficult to know whether you first notice the ball being kicked around or the footballers' tattoos. Then

there's also the hipster's beard, which now seems to be worn a little shorter than before, another international trend which also seems to have increased business for barbers' shops.

Zygmunt Bauman:

Football pitches are the most massively and most regularly attended places in the world today. No wonder that whoever wishes to find a likely solution to the universal concern we are discussing here looks in that direction, investing hopes of coming across reliable, trustworthy choices in the sheer numbers of (dedicated and mostly satisfied) fans.

And what about the body as the increasingly favourite place on which to locate the signs of hope, and the expectation that the insoluble quandary of wedding belonging with self-assertion, and the duration of identity with its flexibility and ability to be manipulated, has been resolved – or at least has come as close to resolution as is conceivable? Outer clothes signal your readiness and ability to renounce the tokens of today's identity in favour of others – and at a moment's notice; they even enable and prove your ability to embody a number of different identities at the same time.

On the other hand, the tokens of denominating decisions engraved/encrusted on the body suggest that the identity they imply – as far as the person is concerned – is a more lasting and more serious commitment, not just a momentary whim. Tattoos signal – miracle of miracles – in one fell swoop, the intentional stability (perhaps even the irreversibility) of a pledge and the freedom to choose to mark the right to self-definition and its exercise.

Thomas Leoncini:

In various parts of the world – and I'm thinking in particular of Africa – a man without scarifications is regarded as a nullity in all respects. As Giorgio Raimondo Cardona wrote in 1981, 'among the Bafia of Cameroon, a man who is not scarred looks like a pig or chimpanzee'. In addition, another key aspect, if we are looking at 'fashions', is how, for many peoples, *transition to manhood* differs from *transition to womanhood*. Manhood has to be conquered, the final attainment after a long test of endurance. Womanhood is an inevitable and routine path, whose final outcome is taken for granted. At least a pass is guaranteed for all women. Faced with sentences like these, we are likely to form a negative opinion of the other face of global culture, a fact that, I think, is only because we forget the cultural relativism that Claude Lévi-Strauss identified as an essential pillar of contemporary anthropology in his *Tristes Tropiques*. Cultural relativism is the approach that tries to understand behaviour and values by looking at them in the overall context in which they are shaped and formed. We are critical at home and anti-conformist in other people's homes, and this explains why, even if we travel to Cameroon and observe practices like ritual scarification, cannibalism and magic rites, we are not too disturbed, because they are practised by the *other*. What's more, we are profoundly influenced by the concept of cultural control (to cite Roger Keesing's theory): we only see and observe the characteristics of the dominant group and hardly ever those of the minority.

Coming back to scarifications and to tattoos, the reasoning is this: the more you suffer to attain your status (and here status is strongly permeated by gender identity), the worthier you are to carry the marks, the more honoured you are to belong. Don't you think that this need to 'cut' your body, knowingly causing pain – which in many respects is akin to flagellation with the aim of attaining a new identity – is comparable, at least unconsciously, to the modern need to get a tattoo?

Zygmunt Bauman:
Yes, I believe you're right – and in more than one respect (although if you wish to search for the mediaeval antecedents of tattooing, look at branding – and even that with due caution – *not* flagellation!).

Over the last few decades, debate regarding the discourse of fashion in respected social sciences and psychology has taken place and been conducted in close connection with the so-called 'embodiment turn'. Indeed, where do the tangled arguments of belonging and individuality, duration and transience – the two formative contradictions that underpin the phenomenon of fashion – find fuller, and at the same time more intrusively visible, manifestations than in our continuous work on the representation of our human *bodies*, or at least in the volume of thought and energy we tend to invest in it?

Thomas Leoncini:

Tattoos and beards, but obviously that's not all. Another pillar of contemporary fashion is the increasingly frequent use of plastic surgery. France Borel's theory regarding its significance in our society has also met with consensus in academic circles: the theory suggests that cosmetic surgery – above all, if used repeatedly – is the most violent and concealed manifestation of the tendency to self-mutilation, hidden under the cloak of official medicine. An individual refuses to accept his or her body as it is, and in parallel also seeks to vent the need for 'self-destruction' (Freud called it the death drive). Under the 'cloak' of official medicine, the theory goes on, a person can satisfy both needs and, at the same time, feel part of the dominant culture, which dictates the creation of a form of beauty that meets set canons identified as the best. The dominant culture is therefore the weapon that, through 'fashion', legitimates the synergy of 'self-destruction' and the 'humanization' of beauty, moving towards the stereotype of an ideal model of beauty.

Zygmunt Bauman:

You take the current crazes of tattooing and

football, aided and abetted by plastic surgery and the beard – never (as yet) definitively shorter or longer – as the key representation of the currents dominating the present-day scenario in the history of fashion, and as the paramount playing field on which the game of fashion is presently experimented, rehearsed and rendered publicly visible and accessible for appropriation and emulation.

Thomas Leoncini:

I'd say that these are the most striking transformations, the ones that most clearly affect a large number of today's 'masses'. Leafing through the latest statistics for cosmetic surgery, produced and circulated by the ASPS (American Society of Plastic Surgeons), the percentage of American adolescents, both boys and girls (aged 13–19 years old), using cosmetic surgery rises by 1 per cent a year.

There are also odd findings: increasing numbers of the young hate their ears. Of all the youngsters who undergo operations, as many as 28 per cent undergo ear plastic surgery, and the trend has been constantly rising by 3 per cent for a number of years now. The ear is rather a particular organ, and two explanations can perhaps be put forward to explain these feelings: one is psychological – but perhaps also a little too metaphysical – (doesn't the ear compel us to listen to others, even when we don't want to?) and the other purely physiological. But what's wrong with the anatomy of the ear?

Zygmunt Bauman:

The supposition that psychologically 'the ear [compels] us to listen to others' seems to me far-fetched and unwarranted. I'd rather focus on the ears being the part of the body sticking out from the rest of it most obtrusively and so also most irritatingly: after all, they obviously do it without asking their owner's permission – let alone at his/her behest. And so, if they depart from the currently preferred model (that is, the one momentarily in fashion), they provide evidence – which is most difficult to overlook – of the owner's demeaning slovenliness and of her/his negligence of the duty of controlling her/his appearance, at least the part that is meant or allowed to be publicly visible.

Thomas Leoncini:

The latest figures for plastic surgery in adults show something different. Since 2000, ASPS has reported a considerable rise in all surgery: breast augmentation surgery is up by 89% (99,614 in 2015, compared to 52,836 in 2000), buttock augmentation up by 252% (4,767 in 2015 compared to 1,356 in 2000), vaginal rejuvenation has increased 3,973% (8,431 in 2015 compared to 207 in 2007). The demands change with age, but the business of plastic surgery appears to be timeless.

Zygmunt Bauman:

There's no business like plastic surgery business . . . The contemporary culture of the society of consumers is ruled by the precept 'If you can do it, you must do it.' The idea of not using the existing opportunities to 'improve' the appearance of your own body (read: bringing it closer to the currently dominating fashion) is made to feel repellent; it tends to be widely viewed as debasing, casting the culprit down in his/her social value and esteem; awareness that this is the case is also, consequently, a humiliating and painful blow to one's self-esteem.

This state of affairs, I repeat, is closely connected with ours being a society of consumers: were the above-mentioned precept not massively and keenly obeyed, the consumerist economy would fall into trouble or perhaps even collapse because of failing to reproduce. Consumerist economy thrives (indeed, survives) thanks to the magical stratagem of recasting possibility into an obligation: in economists' terms, supply into demand. The phenomenon of fashion – in this case, of determining the binding patterns of the body's outer look according to the capabilities of the cosmetic industry and surgical interventions on offer – plays a crucial role in making such miraculous conversion run smoothly.

But, essentially, we are still moving on the same ground we traversed when trying to grapple with issues raised in your first question. Whatever we said about the ultimate sources of the present-day tattoo craze applies as well to the craze of cosmetic surgical/pharmaceutical interventions (by the way, in our world known to substitute fathoming by 'surfing', both crazes operate on the surface of the body and few people if any would declare such curtailment wrong). At the roots of both vogues/rages/infatuations, we would find the dialectics of belonging and self-definition and the logics of fashion and 'embodiment'. One more comment is in order, though. Your figures signal, importantly, unsteadiness, and so the possibility of redirection, even a reversal, of trends. Statistical indices can go up or down (again moved by turns of consumerist-economy markets with their vested interests in conjuring up ever new markets for ever new products meant to gratify ever new needs). What we are recording here are in all probability temporary phenomena – today's modes of manifestation of some more durable trends boasting a longer life-expectancy.

Thomas Leoncini:
A few other points are worth stressing: very young girls today often (increasingly often) boast about having undergone plastic surgery. Until a few years ago, this was not the case – in fact, I think I can say that the trend was quite the opposite. All you need to do is log in to any social network – particularly Instagram, say – and type in the hashtag #lips: you'll find an indirect eulogy of cosmetic surgery, a theatre in which the star performance is the reconstruction of the girl according to the very precise norms and stand-ards of beauty of liquid modernity. If beauty is a

search for humanity, this hypothesis is the proof that the individuality of liquid modernity is trying to establish itself in this field, too. Let me explain: anyone who's proud of their reconstructive surgery aimed at an aesthetic ideal of humanity (almost an aesthetic ideal of community) is truly proud of their own individuality. But I'm talking about that individuality which has allowed the young girl to cannibalize her *individuo de jure*, her individual rights and duties, at the expense of her *individuo de facto*, the individuality that only thinks of her own capacity for self-affirmation.

Might female pride in the act of plastic surgery also be a result of the ostentation of wealth? A demonstration of personal economic status? Might the moment come when girls will measure time through the lens of beauty, and therefore beauty (and also time) might be turned back thanks to surgery . . . ?

Zygmunt Bauman:

How right of you to add to our vision the wealth factor! A flawless, spick-and-span body shape – as much, if not more than, the jackets, tops or skirts purchased in the most reputable (and so also the most expensive) fashion establishments – implies high credit status and a swollen wallet – and, therefore, the superior social position and public esteem which go with them. They proclaim loudly, and in a language widely understood: 'I can afford it, unlike you, poor creature! Draw your own conclusion, know your place and stick to it!!' This, however, seems to me to be a rather supra-gender or gender-neutral factor – and the same relates to the 'very young girls' proud of undergoing plastic surgery similar to the procedures their older sisters or schoolmates have had (a phenomenon akin to 'very young boys' proud of smoking cigarettes in the school latrines – a step towards adulthood of which many, perhaps most, children of both sexes dream, and whose arrival they dearly wish to speed up in order to enjoy the privileges which – as children – they are normally refused). Another, blatantly gender-related factor may and ought to be used, however, in the explanation of the phenomenon you signal. At the time the publishers of *Playboy* were launching *Playgirl* – its intended female-readership counterpart – onto the market, a hot public debate took place about which kind of photos the women clients would look for and prefer to find: the most beautiful specimens of the opposite sex (just as male readers of *Playboy* tend to behave), or the most powerful and influential (in the likely case of the two types of men not coinciding). Hired researchers and the reading public then agreed on the verdict: the second choice was more popular, and so probably the more desirable for women readers, than the first. On the whole, if women tend to score on the scale of desirability by their beauty, men tend to be mostly evaluated on the same scale according to their fitness; assuming that most men prefer their women womanly while most women prefer their partners to be manly, one would indeed expect fitness – both physical fitness and the fitness to confront life's challenges and to protect one's partner against the harms such challenges may cause (by, for example, industry, power, agility, alertness, courage, energy, enterprise, vigour or vitality) – to beat the attractions of a beautiful body surface, hands down. The plastic/cosmetic industry, however, is in these terms aimed at serving female needs and recruiting its clients primarily, even if not exclusively, from the women's half of the population.

Thomas Leoncini:
So the identikit of the ideal man for today's

woman of liquid modernity is a rich man? Is the fashion of wealthy men partnered by attractive, younger women destined to last forever?

Zygmunt Bauman:

Let's not jump to conclusions, Thomas! And no shortcuts in reasoning, please! After all, you base your generalized conclusion on a very narrow – and in addition not random, but self-selected – sample: *Playgirl* readers. My hunch is that it by and large overlaps with the (similarly constricted) aggregate of the clients of the plastic/cosmetic industry; if that hunch is correct, it might go some way towards explaining the huge prevalence of females among those clients, but surely it's not enough for generalizing about 'the identikit of the ideal man' being 'a rich man'. Moreover, on what grounds do you prophesize that it is 'destined to last forever'?!

Thomas Leoncini:

We're talking about girls, about women. And not about boys or men. This is not because men don't resort to cosmetic surgery, but because it's much rarer to find males boasting about having undergone surgery. Why do you think this is? Even when today's boys are aesthetically ambitious, just like girls are – sometimes even more so . . .

Zygmunt Bauman:
Men resorting to its services risk lowering their score on the attractiveness scale.

2

Transformations of aggressivity

Bullying

Thomas Leoncini:

Steven Spielberg, Barack Obama, Rihanna, Miley Cyrus, Kate Middleton, Madonna and Bill Clinton all have something in common: they were bullied at school and were victims of numerous violent attacks. Let's try to analyse bullying by starting from an unusual angle. According to Arnold van Gennep, one of the most respected anthropologists of the twentieth century, the key characteristics of all coming-of-age rites are constructed, assembled and formed around three stages. The first is a period of separation of the individual from the community (known as the *preliminary rite*, which allows the individual to terminate the previous condition). This is followed by the period of marginalization (known as *liminality*) in which there is a genuine suspension of social status – the subject is in a sort of limbo, both in terms of social stability, because he or she can create a *new community spirit*, a *new communitas*, as the Scottish anthropologist Victor Turner argued. You need only realize that many recent anti-conformist social revolutions trace their origins back to situations of liminality: the hippies are now unrecognizable as the forebears of the *punkabbestia*[3] or the Goths, but in turn they are the forebears of emo fans, who today only have the hipsters, perhaps, as a further liminal liquid transformation. The third stage is that of aggregation, technically referred to as the *postliminary rites*, because the subject returns to his or her natural habitat as an integral and newly connected part of the community, but with new individual characteristics that are activated when placed in the social context.

Therefore, separation, marginalization and lastly aggregation. These stages, if we seek them in many situations where the phenomenon of bullying is widespread, are also often representative of the path followed by the victim of bullying. Faced with the bully's attacks, especially if these are repeated, the victim feels psychologically (and often also physically) 'separated' from others.

---

[3] The Italian *punkabbestia* are closely associated to gutter punks, or crusties.

The victim's sense of living apart upsets not only his or her everyday life, often affecting attainment at school, but also relations with loved ones, and all too frequently it leads to a change in friendships, in everyday contacts. It can therefore create a new *minimal nucleus* of social belonging, and this coincides with the phase of marginalization, when – in response to this sense of unease – many victims of bullying devise ways of not having to undergo further suffering by finding themselves another identity, given that the previous one led to so much pain. After (or during) all this, it is inevitable – because society demands it of the victim – that there is a new aggregation: relations with classmates and with the school in general must be re-established so as not to remain behind and to avoid failure and being kept back at school. But at the end of this path, perhaps after a month or so – or, at worst, a few years – the victim of bullying returns to society as a new person, as a person who brings with them a new, more complex social identity.

Can bullying without physical violence be seen as the equivalent of a rite of passage for some youngsters? Are bullies born bullies because bullying forms part of their 'habitus'?

Zygmunt Bauman:

Norbert Elias, the formidable German–British sociologist and social historian, in 1939 memorably unpacked the concept of the 'civilizing process' as referring not so much to the elimination of aggressiveness, undue coercion and violence from human life (that, probably, he considered a downright utopian idea), but as, so to speak, 'sweeping all three of them under a carpet': removing them from the sight of 'civilized people', out of places such people are likely to visit, or all too often even to hear about, and transferring them to the charge of 'inferior people', excluded for all practical intents and purposes from the 'civilized society'. Efforts to achieve such an effect went together with elimination of behaviour which had been recognized, evaluated and condemned as barbaric, coarse, crude, discourteous, ill-bred, ill-mannered, impertinent, impolite, inelegant, loud-mouthed, loutish, rude, unseemly or vulgar – and, all in all, uncouth and unfit to be used by 'civilized persons', and degrading and discrediting them if used. Elias's study was published on the eve of the most barbaric explosion of violence in the history of the human species – but, at the time it was written, the phenomenon of 'bullying' was all but unknown, or at least stayed unnamed. When, in the last decade, violence returned from exile with a vengeance, and vulgar language elbowed out the elegant speech from salons and the public stage, numerous disciples and followers announced the advent of a 'de-civilizing process' and leaned over backward to explain the sudden, unanticipated reversal in the human condition – albeit to little and unsatisfactory – and unconvincing – effect.

More radical voices went somewhat further: they reached back to Oswald Spengler's *The Decline of the West* (*Der Untergang des Abendlandes* in its German original – 'Downfall' being a more faithful translation of the 'Untergang') – suggesting that what is happening currently to the civilization of the West is but another repetition of the pattern each civilization, past and future, must follow in its history. Using his unique botanical metaphors, Spengler presented that pattern as a succession of: Spring, with its bold – because naïve – creativity (George Steiner was to suggest much later that the advantage of Voltaire, Diderot or Rousseau consisted in their ignorance – in not knowing what we, alas, are aware of); Summer, with its maturation of flowers and fruits; Autumn, with their wilting and fading; and, finally, Winter, marked by the freezing of the creative spirit in half-dead – anything but creative – mannerisms. As for the case of the West, the passage from (spiritual) culture to mundane, material, matter-of-fact civilization occurred around 1800:

> on the one side of that frontier life in fullness and sureness of itself, formed by growth from within, in one great uninterrupted evolution from Gothic childhood to Goethe and Napoleon, and on the other the autumnal, artificial, rootless life of our great cities, under forms fashioned by the intellect. [. . .] Culture-man lives inwards. Civilization-man outwards in space and amongst bodies and 'facts'.[4]

So there is a choice that can and needs to be made between interpretive offers descending from the sophisticated/sublime – and in their intentions, universalistic – heights of *Geschichtephilosophie*. In our conversation, however, we are pursuing nearer-to-earth-and-to-the-prose-of-daily-life, mundane and to a great extent localized factors, prompting

---

[4] Oswald Spengler, *The Decline of the West: Form and Actuality*, trans. Charles Francis Atkinson, New York: Alfred A. Knopf, 1927, p. 353.

and shaping up the current developments in our culture, mind-set and behavioural patterns.

Thomas Leoncini:
And in our modernity, where do you think cultural development is going?

Zygmunt Bauman:
At the moment, the development you suggest pursuing is the return of violence, coercion and oppression to the resolution of conflicts, at the expense of argument and of dialogue aimed at mutual understanding and the re-negotiation of *modus co-vivendi*. I guess that an important role in this development has been played, continues to be played and will still be played in the foreseeable future by the new technology of mediated communication – not as its cause, but as its crucial enabling condition.

Thomas Leoncini:
The first testimonial comes from Michele, who's now thirty years old:

I still have nightmares. I was very shy and solitary. Three of my classmates locked me in the toilets and started to beat me up, first with their hands, and then with brooms and anything else that happened to be in the room. Five interminable, humiliating and painful minutes. While two of them laid into me, the other one undid his trousers and pissed on me. Even today, I start crying when I think about that day, not only because of my humiliation at the time, but because the next day, together with my father, I told the head teacher what had happened. He put his hand on my shoulder, though, and said that these things happen, that unfortunately today's boys are like that, but these situations don't last, and I shouldn't worry because everything would be better in the days to come (one of the three was the son of a well-known doctor, a very wealthy man in the city). But obviously the bullying didn't stop there and it continued for the rest of the school year.

Michele's story reveals the double-edged sword of bullying: the same blade that makes the first, deep wound then inflicts new pain, as if the first were not enough, when it is withdrawn from the flesh. The head teacher of the school (who does not understand what Michele is suffering) then causes the boy's social exclusion. Have you ever been bullied?

Zygmunt Bauman:
In answer to your question: yes, I was. Permanently, daily. Throughout my schooling in Poznan, Poland, until my escape from my hometown at the outbreak of war. In the company of the other two Jewish boys among the pupils. Obviously, I wasn't then a trained sociologist, but I remember understanding quite well that being bullied was a matter of exclusion. You are not like us, you do not belong, you have no right to join our games, we won't play with you; if you insist on sharing in our life, don't be puzzled by all that beating, kicking, offending, degrading and debasing.

Much later I understood, once I started reading sociology books and learned to think sociologically, that the exclusion of three Jewish boys in the several-hundred-pupil-strong school was, for our persecutors, the flip-side of the coin of their self-identification. Somewhat later still, I followed the novelist E. M. Forster's advice – 'only connect';[5] it dawned on me that appointing an enemy and proving his inferiority, by hook or by crook, was the inseparable second face of

[5] This is the epigraph to *Howards End*.

the self-identification coinage. There wouldn't be 'us' were there no 'them'. But fortunately for making real our wish to stay together, to like each other and help each other, there are 'them' and therefore there are – there need to be – 'us', manifesting our togetherness in word and deed and never tiring of reminding ourselves of it and demonstrating – reaffirming – proving it to others around. For all practical intents and purposes, the idea of 'us' would be meaningless if not coupled with 'them'.

That rule, I am afraid, does not bode well for the dream of a world free of bullying.

Thomas Leoncini:

So you're talking about exclusion. This is precisely what the second testimonial powerfully highlights: the feeling of being excluded.

Laura is fifteen years old and, unlike Michele, she's not yet freed herself from the problem of bullying, as she herself admits:

I don't want to go to school because my companions make me feel different. I'd like to be like them, but they won't let me. If I dress like them, they laugh at me; if I imitate what they do, they mock me. My classmates call me a loser, and say I'll never have any friends, let alone a boyfriend. I'm starting to think they're right. I don't know why they hate me so much, but I know it makes me feel terrible (this way of being excluded). I often think about suicide as a solution to my pain.

Male bullying seems to differ in many respects from female bullying. For example, in most cases, physical violence is used among males, while among females verbal violence is far more common, often coupled with silence as a form of isolation.

According to the latest figures from NCES (National Center for Education Statistics),[6] one out of five American students is a victim of bullying and, as various international studies show,

[6] This is the Federal organization for the collection and analysis of education data in the United States and in other nations. NCES forms part of the Institute of Education Sciences, in the US Department of Public Education. This body fulfils a mandate of Congress to collect, compare, analyse and report full statistics on the state of education in America; it carries out and publishes surveys and reports on international educational activities. The up-to-date figures for the study of bullying cited here were published in late December 2016 and can be consulted online at https://nces.ed.gov/pubs2017/2017015.pdf.

one of the key 'motives' for picking on a student is his actual or presumed homosexuality. These studies also reveal more: gay boys and lesbian girls are three times more likely to commit suicide than their other peers.

This risk was expressly mentioned a few years ago by the United States Department of Health and Human Services (HHS) in Washington.[7] What's your view of all of this?

Zygmunt Bauman:
Personally, I wouldn't make too much of the arguments that male and female bullies, respectively, advance to explain their bullying of their chosen victims. Arguments come and go following current fashions, but unpleasantnesses of life stay and obtrusively demand to be unloaded, letting off the accumulated steam and preventing the new from accumulating. Demand for bullying, and above all for its objects and reasons, hardly ever goes to sleep – and, indeed, it never

[7] This is the Federal government department responsible for the health of American citizens. Its various tasks include the administration of public health services and the overseeing of private health provision, monitoring the prevention of diseases, and operating the Food and Drug Administration.

did. At one time, life's bitterness blamed demonic possession; then, unsuccessful marriage or lack of orgasms; later still, it was sexual exploitation and abuse by parents; currently, it's childhood sexual harassment by teachers, priests and – best of all – celebrities; now you homosexuals are the culprit – but you forgot to mention the migrants, currently leaving every other pretender far behind . . .

Thomas Leoncini:

The migrants. Of course, Zygmunt, you're right. Another distinct problem facing us today. Well over 200 years ago, Immanuel Kant made a very straightforward comment, which I've heard you mention several times: he wondered what the practical consequences of the earth's spherical surface might be. The most evident of all, for us who are born on this planet, is that we live on the surface of this sphere. But let's try to imagine what it might mean to 'travel', to 'move' from one point of a sphere to another. Above all, it increasingly 'shortens' the distances between us and others. This is because by moving across the sphere, we are simply narrowing the distance between us and others which, by moving, we had initially attempted to enlarge. Kant continued this train of thought by remarking that, sooner or later (although given that he wrote over two centuries ago, we can think of ourselves now as being in both the 'sooner' and the 'later'), the time will come when there will be no more empty spaces where those who regard the places already populated by their fellows as too uncomfortable, too crowded, can venture. What these comments reveal is that it is logical to accept the imposition made by Nature and view hospitality as a founding pillar of modernity.

Going back to the topic we were talking about, bullying, the story of Kitty Genovese comes to mind; more than being about indifference, it is a story that is often used as an example in social psychology to emphasize how people tend to shift personal responsibility onto the level of collective social responsibility, forgetting that in everyday life people are influenced by a strong sense of individuality and this affects their social relations. Kitty Genovese was a woman from New York who was stabbed to death close to her home, in Kew Gardens, which is in the Queens neighbourhood. It happened in 1964, and the next day the *New York Times* dedicated the main front page headline to the subject: '37 who saw Murder didn't call the Police'.

To put it bluntly, what is the conclusion? Here it is: a single witness to a tragic event, realizing he is alone, is more likely to go to the aid of the victim than an individual who realizes that he is with others, with a collective presence of other people.

Without going into too much detail about the story and the controversy that it sparked (searching for the truth, Kitty Genovese's brother later pointed out a number of mismatches between the newspaper reports and what actually happened), the message is clear: pluralism often seems to bring about a change, even if a transient one – a change in individuality, making it lighter. The end result doesn't change: a poor woman massacred in the middle of the street by a madman, while those who lived nearby (probably) watched the scene from behind the curtains; no one came out, no one rang the police for half an hour, in spite of the victim's screams. The lights were on, and silhouetted figures watched from behind closed windows, spreading the responsibility to act (you're watching too, not just me, so why should I do anything if you don't?), and this inevitably diminishes the personal impact that triggers the response to help. Is that day in 1964 one of your most powerful memories?

Zygmunt Bauman:
Yes, I, so to speak, 'lived through' that case, through the shock that reverberated through the enlightened opinion of that time – far beyond the academic realm, forced to revise more than one of its tacitly or explicitly held views. If I remember correctly, during the debate that followed and went on for a length of time unusual for moral panics, I heard for the first time of the concept of the 'bystander' – a person who witnesses evil being done but turns their eyes the other way and does nothing to stop it.

That concept struck me immediately as perhaps by far the most important category among those absent from the studies of genocide but crying for admission. It took me, however, two decades to give it the justice it deserved in my own attempt to crack the mystery of the holocaust conducted at the peak of the modern civilization. (Genovese was murdered in 1964, at the threshold of what was perceived as a cultural revolution re-evaluating all values – as the 1960s were soon to become recorded in the annals of cultural history – and before learned attention found another topic on which to focus; as the psychologist Gordon Allport once caustically – and only partly tongue-in-cheek – put it, we in human sciences never solve issues, we only get bored with them ... What Allport neglected to mention, however, was that not every problem has a solution; many don't – and gratuitous murders like Genovese's belong to that category. Policemen who, as we learn from detective films, seek motives in the first place, have an impossible task to perform – and so do the prosecutors, and the jury, and the judges.)

But we may say retrospectively, with the benefit of later insights, that the Genovese case brought to the surface one more phenomenon destined to acquire more and more sombre importance in the years that followed, and yearning to be caught in the conceptual net: that of 'random evil', or 'disinterested evil'. At his trial, the perpetrator, Winston Moseley – the murderer – told the jury that he chose a woman rather than a man for a victim simply because women 'were easier and didn't fight back'.

The cynicism and aimlessness of 'random'

or 'gratuitous' evil escape understanding and 'rational', 'cause-and effect' explanations, which in our modern way of thinking it must possess. That one of its qualities constitutes the topic central to the films of the great screenwriter and film director Michael Haneke, one of the most dedicated and thorough explorers and chroniclers of that shatteringly puzzling variety of evil. Luisa Zielinski, interviewing Haneke for the Winter 2014 issue of the *Paris Review*, so summarized his cinematographic work: 'His camera omits the brains-on-the-windshield clichés and torture porn of Hollywood. It lights, instead, on the everyday cruelties to which audiences are not yet numb: the petty acts of bullying, the failure to listen, the delusions of class and privilege.'[8] Already in May 2001, Peter Bradshaw opined Haneke's *Code Unknown* to be a 'dazzling, uncompromising film impossible to pin down'. But, I would say, this is because the ways and means of its cast's mode of being in the world, which Haneke puts on display deliberately (and

---

[8] The interview is available online at https://www.the parisreview.org/interviews/6354/michael-haneke-the-art-of-screenwriting-no-5-michael-haneke.

prudently!) unaccompanied by comments, let alone explanations, are precisely like that: they are 'impossible to pin down'. A message returning over and over again in one after another of Haneke's films – recently restated by the daughter of the interminably ill mother just strangled by her husband in her five-minute-long silence in the last scene of *Amour* ... In my own inept way, nothing like Haneke's mastership in expressing the inexpressible, saying the unsayable, articulating the inarticulable and rendering the un-intelligible intelligible, I summoned the unique insightfulness of my late colleague and dear friend Leonidas Donskis to jointly tackle the same mystery in our *Liquid Evil* and *Moral Blindness*.

Novel, unfamiliar, heretofore un-noted (let alone mentally and emotionally assimilated) events tend to shock simply because they are such. Similar events, when repeated, multiplying and watched or heard of daily, tend to be stripped of their shocking capacity. However appalling and horrifying they might have been at their first appearance within sight, they become, through the monotony of their repetition, 'normalized', made 'ordinary' – things just as things are by their nature; in other words, they are trivialized, and the function of trivia is to amuse and entertain, rather than shock.

In 2011, Anders Behring Breivik committed two mass murders: one targeting the government and contingent civilian population, the other against the inmates of a summer camp run by the Workers' Youth League (AUF). He explained his crimes in advance in an electronically published manifesto sounding the alarm against Islam and feminism joining forces in 'creating a European cultural suicide'. He also wrote that his main *motive* for the outrage was to '*market* his manifesto'. We may say that Breivik appealed here to the present-day common sense: the more scandalous and dire the advertising copy, the higher the TV ratings, the newspaper sales or box-office profits it may generate. What strikes a thoughtful reader, nevertheless, is the total absence of a logical link between the cause and effect: Islam, feminism on one side, and the random victims of mass murder on the other.

We are being quietly adjusted to this logic-defying, indeed mind-boggling, state of affairs. Breivik is anything but an exceptional, one-off blunder of nature, or a solitary monster without likes and progeny: the category of which he is a member is notorious for recruiting ever new members through the mechanism known as the 'copycat'. Look, for instance, around American campuses, schools and public gatherings; watch the terrorist and other violent acts incessantly screened on TV; check the repertoire of cinemas near you, or browse through the successive lists of bestselling books, to see how much we are daily exposed to the sights of random, gratuitous, unmotivated violence – violence for its own sake, and no other. Evil has been fully and truly trivialized, and what really counts among the consequences is that we have been, or are rapidly being, made insensitive to its presence and manifestations. Doing evil no longer demands motivation. Has it not – bullying included – been shifting in its great part from the class of purposeful (indeed, meaningful) actions to the space of (for a growing number of bystanders) pleasurable pastime and entertainment?!

3

Transformations of sex and dating

Declining taboos in the era of finding love online

Thomas Leoncini:

We regret the past only because we know we can't go back there. Practically every day you hear someone talking about the good old days as being 'fairer' – a time when things were as they should be. And then you go to the bar or glance at a newspaper, and you find a recurrent theme in all these non-places:[9] youngsters aren't enjoying their youth, because of the Internet and smartphones.

---

[9] These are the opposite of anthropological places. They were defined by the contemporary French ethnologist and anthropologist Marc Augé as *non-lieux*, and they are not concerned with identity or history and cannot be defined as relational. According to Augé, our supermodernity (*surmodernité*) is filled with them. They include transit points and temporary abodes (like hotels), as well as shopping malls. They are representative of, and quantify, an era. Augé wrote that the traveller's space may be the archetype of non-place. From a more technical viewpoint, a non-place designates two complementary but distinct realities: spaces formed in relation to certain ends (transport, transit, commerce, leisure) and the relations that individuals have with these spaces (*Non-places: Introduction to an Anthropology of Supermodernity*, London and New York: Verso Books, 1995, p. 94).

Everyone's ready to accuse them of being constantly online, always looking at their phones, of carrying with them what is, by definition, the most modern and liquid non-place (the web) and of living in a pocket limbo. It's a place that doesn't exist, where a steady stream of relationships is created, but they too are non-existent: popular legend has it, for instance, that when two youngsters with smartphones actually meet, they talk for a bit and then they go on staring into their phones, building parallel digital universes. Yet, today's kids are just like we were. With a few differences: we grew up chatting on the home phone, and they've grown up at home on their mobile phones! Although, if you think about it, that's not absolutely true. When I was fifteen, it had just become trendy to take a mobile phone into school (it cost over 400,000 lire for a 'portable' phone that was so cumbersome it would only fit into a large pocket; once I remember putting one in the front pocket of my jeans and I found the antenna poking out above my shoes). We also spent the day glued to the phone screen, and some of you may even remember why. Because we received a token call. These one-ring calls were completely undervalued by the media in the early 2000s, but they had the same impact then as WhatsApp for youngsters today. If you fancied a girl, first of all you had to make sure she had a phone, then you had to barter something to get her number, and lastly – and most importantly – you gave her a call, letting her phone ring just once. If nothing happened after that, then the girl was probably one of those who 'was a bit up herself' (we used that phrase without understanding it, but we liked it). Then you gave her another call, but not too many – that would be over the top and you'd end up being insulted by her boyfriend. With luck, a text message would pop up, one that had been eagerly anticipated and could make your summer come alive simply because it brought with it an unexpected waft of fresh air. And do you know what it said? Quite simply: 'Who are you?' That's how you knew what sort she was; and you had to choose whether to tell the truth or pretend to be someone else, even if you could be sure that, having received the call, the girl had already double-checked with all her girlfriends to see whether they knew someone with that number. From then on, you spent day after day checking your phone, hoping to see that little envelope appear on the screen, even if you could barely read it in the sun.

This brings me to an aspect that undoubtedly marks a 'continuation' compared to now: namely, the fact that youngsters then, like those of today, were particularly interested in anything that could shorten distances and accelerate how they selected and recruited sexual partners, allowing time to prevail over space in every respect. WhatsApp, Telegram, Snapchat, Messenger – all do this to an extraordinary degree: they save time, they let us reach our goal sooner, they are instant processes that sanction, as never before, the end of spatial distances, leaving time as the only slender barricade. The question is always put like this: 'How long would it take me to join you in Miami if I'm in Rome?' Have you ever heard anyone say: 'How many kilometres do I have to travel in order to get to you?' Liquid modernity has completely altered our psychological frameworks and, as a result, our kinaesthetic prototypes. But what does the web really mean for us and our identities? Is it a completely different world, or something that is now an indispensable adjunct for our identity? There are countless cases in which the Internet, by acting as a showcase for human identity, has left victims in its web of connections: in fact, so many suicides have resulted from insidious but violent assaults upon particularly fragile individuals. We need not bother to add to the already appalling reputation of Ask.fm, a website that allows users to write anything without revealing their own identity; you get a clear idea if you stop to consider, for instance, the large number of cases of cyber attacks and defamation. For certain, there is one distinctive, universal trait that is true of everything on the web: the public sphere is belittled to the advantage of the private one. But this is precisely what undermines the *political* significance of the citizen. Yet, with its social networks, the web deludes us into thinking that we can actually mould and spread a universal democracy through our 'likes' and comments. Instead, we are simply creating a personal, individual vision, which is accreted to other different individual visions. And, once again, we bring the private into the public. Often, we imagine our comments on social media to be like rivers made up of the same droplets of water, while on the contrary a better image would be a lake whose surface is covered by countless drops of oil that cannot blend with the water but only demonstrate our individual existence and have no real influence. Yes, these droplets are similar, but not similar enough. And what happens when we observe all of this from the outside? What is the most common way of discrediting this immense flow in just three words? It is to call it 'the online population' (a phrase used by Italian media outlets practically every day), as if these views really belong to a group who are completely extraneous to the real community, ignoring the fact that they are one and the same, and identifying them as a voice that actually (indeed, factually) exists. Yet we see the web not only as an ideal habitat, but also as a political and democratic one. What instead seems shocking is its close resemblance to totalitarian-ism rather than to democracy. Indeed, while the circulation of news and images in real time – what we might call the 'life of the sleeping spectator' – certainly rests on solid democratic foundations, the organization of our personal sphere on the web, namely that of 'active' spectators – or, to put it in other words, our relationships and our open-ness to or rejection of others – is not democratic at all.

Quite the opposite. Through our personal pro-files on social networks, we are all playing with the illusion of totalitarianism: we are free to block individuals, or to delete requests simply because we don't know someone personally. Until a short while ago, Facebook made it possible to report a user who'd sent a friendship request to someone they did not know personally. In this case, the only charge levied against the unfortunate person sending a request to be admitted to another user's digital sanctuary – for which they risked having their account blocked – was that of having asked a stranger to welcome them among their 'friends'. On social media, it only takes a minute or so to set up a fake profile and then to use it to insult other users, all the time sheltered by the infrangible shield of privacy.

The American psychologist Philip Zimbardo carried out an experiment involving two groups of female students, one of which was given ano-nymity by donning hoods and cloaks like those of the Ku Klux Klan, while the second wore ordi-nary clothing. Both groups were then asked to administer an electric shock to another person, and the results showed that the hooded students pressed the button for twice as long, compared to those whose faces were clearly visible.

The power of the phenomenon of deindividu-ation was again confirmed by Zimbardo in his famous experiment in Stanford prison. As another American psychologist, Ed Diener, wrote, by reducing self-consciousness, deindividuation limits access to internal norms of behaviour.

The Internet really gives us the illusion of being unique individuals and being able to manage such copious amounts of information in search of the meaning of life.

Zygmunt Bauman:

You've sketched it in a nutshell, giving a brief but eventful history of the web. Indeed, a combination of great expectations and frustrated hopes seems, in retrospect, its trademark. As you rightly suggest, the web marched into our world under the banner of creating 'an ideal habitat', one that is both political and democratic – but where it helped us to arrive is the present-day crisis of democracy and deepening political and ideological divisions and animosities. We've enthusiastically embraced the promised chance of being born again – but the world in which we tend to conduct our second life is one of cyber attacks and defamation. And, yes, the advent of the web suddenly made our hopes of notoriety realistic, but having put it deceptively within reach made them all but obligatory – though with a chance of fame equal to that of winning the jackpot in a lottery.

But let me start from the beginning and then go through your query point by point. I propose to start with the genuinely seminal departure in the human condition that brought the technology of informatics step by step, in the frame of but one generation, from gigantic constructions – of which, as its inventors and pioneers calculated and anticipated, about a dozen will require to be installed in order to satisfy the totality of mankind's informatics needs – to the myriads of ultimately portable, fist-size gadgets we have today (laptops, tablets, phones, and whatever else could've been 'thrown on the market' before we've finished our conversation); at all times, 24/7, within reach of the billions of their owners/users of all ages on the night-, breakfast- or dinner-tables, in pockets or bags, though most of the time in the hand. However lonely we may be and/or feel, in the online world, we are potentially always in touch. The offline world, however, neither vanished nor is likely to in the foreseeable future; to that offline world, by contrast with the online newcomer marked as 'offline', the above facility does not apply – as it didn't when that world was the only world we inhabited, and its companion/adversary not yet invented – that is, for the most (thus far, almost the whole) of human history.

But now there are TWO worlds; they are starkly distinct from each other – entities fully and truly poles apart, and the job of reconciling them and forcing them to overlap is among the skills that the art of 21st-century life demands we learn, appropriate and use. Different precepts and rules of behaviour, differently drawn lines between 'what one should do' and 'from doing which, one should abstain', and different languages and behavioural codes recommended, used, taught and learned. And yet we are bound to inhabit both – splitting thereby our hours, days (and lives?) between two distinct universes, two behavioural codes, as well as two modes of cohabitation and interaction. 21st-century humans are two-worlds humans. To one of the two – the offline world – we belong. The second – the online world, which we are prompted, repeatedly told and nudged to compose using our own ways and means, while deploying the tools, stratagems and expedients supplied by information technology – is often proclaimed, and all too often experienced, as if it belonged to us. I can – at any rate, in part – design its shape and contents; I can cut out and dispose of its unwanted, inconvenient and uncomfortable fragments; I can monitor performance and get rid of things that failed to meet the standards I set for them. To cut a long story short: online, unlike offline, it is I who am in control – I am the lord, I rule. Maybe I don't pay the piper – but I set the tune. Some witty observer compared that blissful feeling to the one likely to overwhelm a boy left alone in a chocolate shop. The problem, though, is: which of the titbits the boys have found themselves are they likely to pick up and enjoy? Here, dear Thomas, the majority opinion (that access to the Internet will create 'an ideal habitat, but also . . . a political and democratic one', as you put it) has met with bitter disappointment. Access to the Internet is not tantamount to the race for more enlightenment, opening wider horizons, getting acquainted with faiths and attitudes of which you've not been heretofore aware and engaging with them in a dialogue which the 'ideal democratic habitat' calls for. Most social research shows that a majority of Internet users are drawn to use it through attraction to the opportunity not so much of *access*, as of *exit*. The second opportunity has thus far proved more tempting; it is widely used to build shelters, rather than to break down walls and open windows: to cut a 'comfort zone' for oneself out of the confusion of the hurly-burly, disorderly life-world and its challenges to understanding and spiritual tranquillity; to prevent the need to converse with people who hold to opinions that are vexing and upsetting, through being different and poorly comprehended – and so the necessity to engage in an argument and risk defeat. By the simple expedient of deleting from the network or barring access to unwelcome guests, the Internet allows a 'splendid isolation' which in the offline world is purely and simply unattainable and inconceivable (just try to attain the same in the street, neighbourhood, workplace . . .). Instead of serving the cause of extending the volume and raising the quality of human integration, mutual understanding, cooperation and solidarity, the Internet has facilitated practices of enclosure, separation, exclusion, enmity and strife.

And then you raise another tremendously important issue: 'cyber attacks and defamation' . . . The Internet, indeed, provides a free-for-all space for innuendoes, maligning, slander and defamation – and, all in all, for falsehood (as a former Soviet dignitary caustically remarks in his memoirs *Requiem for my Mother Country*, the 'democratic' revolution in Russia 'liquidated the ruling party's monopoly on lies'). You may never meet your victim face-to-face (and vice versa); you stay hidden inside the armour of anonymity; the risk of penalty for calumny is reduced to a minimum.

Thomas Leoncini:

So it is this relationship between 'notoriety' and the web that gives greater resonance to liquid modernity: it's like a rich array of delicacies that makes your mouth water! The web itself is a feast of delights.

Often it is the Internet that amplifies both sexual desires and the desire for immortality. Plato, who was born more than 2,400 years ago, said that man would be shocked by the behaviour of his fellows if he was unable, first of all, to realize that every individual has an innate love of fame and a burning desire for everlasting glory. According to Plato, in order to ensure his reputation in society, a man would face up to any danger, with even greater ferocity than he might use to defend his children.

Everyone has at least ten minutes' celebrity in their life today: you need only make your birthday public on Facebook and you'll be sure to receive a stream of notifications, which for women will often take the form of invitations to meet up for coffee, while for men they'll offer a broader choice of dating opportunities. What do you think about this?

Zygmunt Bauman:
I think this is another important item you rightly bring into our exchange – a novelty which, for a change, may indeed, under better conditions, generate new chances for public life. What you call 'celebrity' is, after all, a two-edged sword. Celebrities are known mostly for being known and talked about, but also persons generating the most beneficial ideas must earn a name for themselves if they wish their propositions to be read, listened to and seriously debated. The Internet dismantles many a barrier built in the past around entry to the public sphere, which all too often amounted to an informal censorship. One wouldn't be able to appear in the public view without earning favours from a TV company; one wouldn't reach the reading public to convey one's own ideas, however original and valuable they might be, unless the board of a respectable newspaper or periodical

agreed to print and distribute them. Such closure or severe constraints imposed on access to the public sphere are by now all but implausible; judging from our exchange – for better or worse . . .

Thomas Leoncini:

According to a recent study by *The Wrap*, an online publication in Hollywood, it is alarming how many post-reality-TV contestants want to commit suicide after the show: there have been eleven deaths of this kind recently in the USA. The magazine writes that contestants don't realize how much stress they'll have to deal with while they're in the limelight. And the victims are the ones you might least expect: the article mentions a deputy district attorney, a single father, a young boxer. Above all, according to *The Wrap*, the phenomenon is not limited just to America, and there are reports of suicides or attempted suicides in India, Sweden and the UK. A recent article in the *New York Post* asserts that it would be worth setting up mental health helplines in America for reality-TV contestants!

Anyone can become famous now if they're in the right place, even a housewife, or millions of cooks dotted all over the world. They are all

people who are not used to being in the spot-
light and they are immediately affected by a very
modern disorder: anxiety. The case of Susan
Boyle was just a drop in the ocean: while wait-
ing for the final of *Britain's Got Talent*, she was
treated for being overstressed. She was diagnosed
with 'television' syndrome: an excess of tension
caused by being catapulted from a completely
normal, even humdrum, life to public acclaim in
front of millions of viewers.

These findings are perfectly in line with the
results of a scientific experiment carried out in
Sweden, by the Karolinska Institutet, which offer
food for thought. A group of 125 volunteers were
asked to try out what is perhaps the perfect – if
impossible – remedy for overcoming anxiety and
panic attacks: invisibility.

Yes, that's right, the remedy consists of convincing yourself that your body is invisible in stressful
social situations. By using a virtual-reality visor,
the volunteers were able to perceive their body as
being completely transparent. The display showed
the space and the objects around their body, but
not the body itself. This perception was reinforced
by touch: the subjects could feel objects touch-
ing their skin but at the same time perceived the

objects as floating in empty space. Then, when the volunteers were confronted by a virtual crowd of people, all staring at them, the ones who had experienced what it felt like to be invisible recorded lower heart rates and stress levels.

Anxiety and depression are much higher in liquid modernity, but the Epicurean need for invisibility has almost disappeared. Yet invisibility might prove to be a cure for these two disorders, typical of liquid modernity. This might seem strange, given that today invisibility is regarded as the worst possible modern social 'illness'. If you're not visible online, you'll have very little chance of scaling the social pyramid – and, above all, you'll have no hope of finding love online. The relationship between sex and love among the young has never been so tenuous in our society. The old concept of the man who did the courting and the woman who was the prey is now seen as an archaic, almost ridiculous, mirage. The new generations of women have transformed the feminine role: today it's the 'female' who is increasingly dominant and acts as the leader in the choice of a partner. Countless young women don't bother to hide the fact that they use online dating and other social media to manage their everyday lives in search of love and friendship.

Zygmunt, has matriarchy been reinstated by today's dominant young women?

Zygmunt Bauman:

Neither matriarchy, it seems, nor patriarchy is the mark of current times – rather, an ongoing negotiation and re-negotiation of male and female roles, under the impact of either history or biography or both factors: roles now set loose, unfixed, let alone cemented, once and for all, 'for better or worse in richer and poorer, till death do us part'. Those roles are now perpetually ill-at-ease in the form they carry at the moment, and thus unconfident in the wisdom of their choice and restless, while perpetually unsure of their alternatives and choices that might be preferred; in other words – uncertainty all around. Most importantly, many – perhaps the majority of – young men and women prefer them in practice to be so, even if they don't express that preference in so many words. They prefer the present-day state of affairs (its flexibility, its being forever non-ultimate and open to re-negotiating) not because they find it convenient (let alone flawless!) – but because they fear its alternatives yet more. Many times, over many years, I repeated that there are two values equally important, indeed indispensable, to decent, gratifying and dignified human life: security and freedom – but that their reconciliation, delivering them each in the satisfactory measure at the same time, is an uphill struggle. You cannot add to your security without detracting from your freedom – and you can't gain more freedom without surrendering something from your security.

Thomas Leoncini:

LovePlus is a Nintendo game that has been around since 2009, and it simulates the experience of romantic love with an adolescent. For many, however, this is not all, and it has become something more: a relationship that is closer to a 'normal' love story. LovePlus has not been marketed very intensely in Europe, but in Japan – if we are to believe the numbers – it's a bestseller in this category. Of the hundreds of thousands of Japanese men who have bought it, many say that they truly love the female avatar created as a 'personal exclusive' of the game; and feedback reveals complete satisfaction with all aspects of their relationship with the young woman. Possession, power, fusion and disenchantment: is virtual love the all-powerful, hypermodern weapon of the Four Horsemen of the Apocalypse?

Zygmunt Bauman:

At the moment of falling in love, you won't probably settle for a one-night stand: you'd want more, much more – you want that love, the wondrous gift of fate to last forever (as elated Johann Wolfgang Goethe shouted, having fallen in love with the sight of his own creation: 'You are so beautiful! *Do not pass away!*) – you no longer can imagine a world that doesn't contain it or living in such a world. The snag is that wishing 'to last forever' means, at least at that moment, no less than a resolution and a promise to one's partner and to oneself of eternal love. And you decide from now on to swim against the current. After all, you make that commitment, that obligation, in a kind of world dedicated to catching fast-passing, short-lived and eminently revocable opportunities; to jumping fences with little if any hesitation the moment you discover that the grass on its other side is greener than on your own. And you are a creature of such a world – you have been brought up, educated, drilled and groomed, as well as reconfirmed daily, to be such a creature. Is there a way to reconcile 'love till death do us part' with the alertness, watchfulness, vigilance and fence-jumping skills, and all-in-all restlessness, of such a creature of such a society?

Thomas Leoncini:
Alertness and watchfulness, do you know what they remind me of? Of desire. That driving force which, by definition, humans idealize in a positive sense, even if it has the potential to wreak havoc. But, to some extent, love and desire can co-exist. As you yourself have explained, destruction forms part of the very essence of desire. Desire is an impulse that destroys – or, rather, an impulse of self-destruction. Love, on the other hand, is the desire to protect the object you cherish. You have defined love as a centrifugal impulse, the opposite of desire, which is centripetal. If desire wishes to consume, love wishes to possess. Love is a threat to the object of its own love, and this is an important point in common with desire. Desire is self-destructive, but the protection that love weaves around the object of its love ends by enslaving the beloved. Love arrests its prisoner and watches over it; it arrests it to protect it. In all this, what is the role of human uncertainty?

Zygmunt Bauman:

The earlier-mentioned uncertainty is the bane of contemporary inter-human bonds (including – and most prominently, as much as painfully – the love relationships). Uncertainty is doomed to be squeezed in the pincers of two mutually hostile, powerful forces which, in the course of their permanent tension, cannot replenish and reinstate their supplies; this kind of condition appears highly unlikely to go away in a foreseeable future. And no wonder that it is and can only be such, considering it is being constantly pressed to deploy its fighters and armaments on two fronts, each one of those two requiring a different sort of military equipment. All too often, success on one front is paid for with reverses on the other – sometimes verging on a genuine debacle. As a conjunction of *ignorance* (in the sense of being incapable of predicting what the other partner in the bond may decide in response to my gambits, or to what ruse, gimmick or manoeuvre s/he may fancy to resort, when and where) and *impotence* (meaning that when/if taken aback, unwarned and unprepared, surprised and confused, I am constantly at risk of responding inadequately to the novel situation likely to emerge), crowned with the heavy blow delivered to my self-confidence and self-esteem by the *humiliation* of being found not up to the task – the experience of the state of uncertainty tends to rebound in seeking escape from the frailty, brittleness, fissiparousness and, all in all, the infirmity and instability of bonds; more often than not, the escape route – be it found or invented, genuine or putative – boils down to the desperate efforts of bond-fixation. Singed fingers may mitigate the fear of hard-and-fast rules, non-negotiable behavioural codes – even of the still recent abhorrence of long-term oath-taking – while softening the opposition to compromise. At least for a time – until the harsh experience of the past melts, disperses and evaporates from memory, while new harsh experiences rehash the balance between gains and losses. Changes in state of mind and spirit, or personal preoccupations and public concerns, as well as in ideal alternatives to the status quo and popular dreams do not follow a straight line; as I have tried repeatedly to demonstrate, they instead follow a pendulum-like trajectory, moving intermittently between the poles of 'full freedom' and 'full security' (neither of the two poles having ever been reached and neither is likely, or indeed conceivable, in the amenable-to-imagining future). As I believe, dear Thomas, the sketched-above dialectics of scarcity and excess in the annals of security and freedom, as sketched above is the proper conceptual and explanatory frame in which the issues you've raised here – of the changing power relations between women and men – should be placed and analysed.

Relations between genders, empirically given as well as postulated, are nowadays as ambiguous, and all too often as torn apart by internal (and endemic!) contradictions, as the values they are pursuing and the conditions which those values are hoped/expected to install once women attain an equal share in their distribution. Terms such as 'patriarchy' or 'matriarchy', together with their numerous and still-growing kin, are neither here nor there. They confuse much more than they will ever be able to explain.

The stake in contemporary gender-ascribed conflicts and strife is no longer power and domination of one of the two sexes over the other. Feminism is indeed about equality – of social standing, opportunities and prestige, authority and access to the sites 'where decisions are made and the action is' – but its other strand, truly seminal, and hopefully with a chance of gaining prevalence, is the ground on which and by which the degree of female emancipation, and its impact on the nature of the resulting human condition, is to be measured: a society in which women are allowed to perform functions that until now have been (in practice, if not in lip service) a man's reserve – thus keeping on the agenda women's reinforcement and reconfirmation of male hegemony using the usual power dynamics – and one in which an earnest attempt is made to re-evaluate and return the specifically, traditionally and endemically female values, and admit them back from their exile in the area of marginality and derivativity.

Thomas Leoncini:
In liquid modernity, sexuality differs from the past, above all, because of changed taboos. What could not be lived openly yesterday, today can be – indeed, it can even be a symptom of the 'avant-garde', surpassing the 'old', a symptom of capacity and intelligence. Jean Piaget spoke about intelligence as the human capacity to adapt to the environment, whether it is a social or a physical environment. The more 'adapted' you are, the

more others think of you as intelligent. We are in a modern life where boundaries are being constantly expanded as barriers recede, and it is becoming increasingly difficult to define today's sexual limits. I'm thinking of the great Lévi-Strauss: 'The birth of culture coincides with the prohibition of incest.' This phrase seems to suggest: 'Physically (technically) you can do it, but know that you must not do it!' The more time passes, the fewer sexual taboos there are, above all for the youngest in society: on social networks, we also witness daily eulogies to individual sexual freedom. Are there any limits to sexuality today? Will even the taboo against incest be abolished in the future?

Zygmunt Bauman:

As to the link between the adaptive capacity and intelligence, I wouldn't be as sure as you seem to be – and this applies to the totality of the social setting, not just its sexual mores part. All socio-cultural changes are operated by the mechanism of a 'creative destruction', which entails, necessarily, adaptation *and* rebellion: assimilation/accommodation that follows breakthrough/rejection (were you wishing to go deeper into the exploration of the logic and working of this mechanism, there could hardly be better advice than to have a long and close look at the work of Gustav Metzger, who in my view succeeded better than any other artist in the effort to grasp, synthesize and succinctly represent the substance of what he brands 'auto-destructive art'). In the contemporary phase of its history, culture drifts spectacularly to its destructive side – or to privilege the destructive ingredient of creation – with the intention to show, demonstrate and emphasize the volatility, frailty, the endemic instability and transience, and the brevity of all cultural products' life expectancy. More and more, creativity's impulses and urges express themselves in seeking and finding new objects of destruction and new borders to transgress. The volume of the known objects for destroying and known borders still amenable to being transgressed, being by their nature limited, tend to be, however, sooner or later, exhausted. You imply that being in the avant-garde consists today in staying in business – though in contriving/inventing/imagining new targets for the job of destruction, instead of bringing to the abattoir specimens heretofore intact. The idea of using the avant-garde concept in the context of contemporary arts seems to me, however, highly doubtful and unadvisable. 'Avant-garde' is a time-tied concept – that metaphor inspired by military practice suggested a relatively small unit exploring the territory about to become the next target and conquest of the army as a whole; it is – by definition – the site-cleaning unit destined to be followed by the bulk of the armed forces, as much as making that happen. Today, no one anticipates (or wishes, promotes, or as little as considers plausible) such a massive absorption of any of the present and future artistic styles on offer. Avant-garde units – or, for that matter, artistic schools – are not plausible either. In our thoroughly individualized society, artists are expected to be one-man (or woman) bands. Lévi-Strauss counted the prohibition of incest as the birth-act of culture because it was the first case of superimposing human-made distinctions on natural identities/differences between humans. He defined culture as an on-going process of *structuration* – as the crisscrossing of the differentiation of the homogeneous with the homogenization of the differentiated, with the help of a twofold arsenal of prescriptions and taboos. By the way, it is amazing that the oldest taboo in the history of the nature vs culture duel–cooperation proved also to be the longest-binding.

Perhaps you've come across a convincing explanation for such a unique resistance power, resulting in such an exceptional longevity?

Thomas Leoncini:
Obviously, I don't know of any as long-lasting as that against incest. So the greatest taboo of history seems destined to persist even into the future of liquidity. This is something new, something solid, in a context where the boundaries are, by definition, proudly liquid, flexible. As I was writing the word 'flexible', my brain immediately conjured up a *schema* which, as it became a *percept* (I use the word in a technical sense precisely to highlight the subjectivity of the vision and set it completely apart from *distal stimulus*), revealed a parallelism that only someone who is 'born liquid' can share with me, appreciating its immediacy of access. When I think of the lemma 'flexibility', I see the word 'work'. It's no coincidence that our study of work – I'm thinking here about the modern development of work psychology – has changed completely: what is key today is to understand and evaluate the gap between formalized (school/academic) knowledge and concrete (practical) knowledge.

What is emerging at a global level is a wider circulation of formalized knowledge (the educational level is undoubtedly higher than in the past), but the formalization of knowledge is not keeping pace with capacity, with the art of knowing how to manage the practice, turning formalized knowledge into everyday practice. I call it art (which will probably bring the critics down on me) because it is a capacity that is subjective and, at the same time, creative – a knowingly creative ability that is very difficult to reproduce exactly in different individuals. So, in working terms, there are many individuals with high-level formal skills who expect others to offer them the possibility of a job, as was the case in the past – specifically in solid modernity, which, broadly speaking, we can say was about 100 years ago – for anyone who had lower formal skills. The result is an excessive and 'de-responsibilized' demand for work (now that I've studied for so long, I deserve a well-paid job, so you, company, give me a well-paid job, tell me what I have to do and how many hours I have to work a day, and I'll do it), which is completely the opposite to the main characteristic of today's job market: flexibility. Our liquid era asks us – those who are born liquid – for just one thing: to be experts in flexibility. And in order to be really useful for working purposes, our formalized knowledge must be aimed in this direction. But, speaking in obligatory generic terms, working flexibility does not meet with the approval of today's young generations, because it calls for a strong sense of responsibilization: we've moved from work as a means of living comfortably and being able to keep ourselves, to work as a means of finding another job – indeed, perhaps a better-paid one. And the search for a comfortable life through work, given that it no longer has a solid point of reference, like stability, is becoming more and more of a distant mirage.

Today, a prolific working life is based above all on the mobilization of skills – in particular, the skills needed to deal with new situations. Keeping up with these transformations is not only complicated for a person who is born liquid, it is also deemed unfair, because it is a characteristic of the lifestyle of someone with a stable, well-paid job – therefore, someone typical of solid modernity. What does all this have to do with how sexuality is perceived in liquid modernity? The answer is a lot. Because, while the liquid generations have not yet adapted on a large scale to working flexibility, it is also true that (in large numbers) these same liquid generations have become professionals of sexual flexibility. Solid love used to be based on eternal love (even if we know how fleeting a promise can seem twenty years later); liquid love is based on the next 'eternal' twenty-four hours. To go on talking in large numbers, the psychological contract between partners today – namely, the implicit undertaking that endows a minimal nucleus with reciprocal expectations and anticipations – is changing in comparison to the past. 'Let me be flexible, give me the freedom to go and I will be even more sincere and free to come back to you.' This change has not happened overnight.

Zygmunt, do you think that working flexibility can really change for those who are born liquid? Will they too be able to find satisfaction through their flexible work? Or is the individual who is born liquid destined to be an unhappy worker? Does flexible love form part of human DNA? I'm thinking about polygamy: many scientists have argued that humans were born polygamous. If this is true, then is liquid love a throwback to the origins of human sexuality?

Postscript

The last lesson

'I wonder what Zyg has written this morning . . . ?' This was the thought that came to me first thing every morning. It seems incredible, but it's true. He was an early riser, although he sometimes burnt the midnight oil too: between seven and eight in the morning was when his comments were most likely to arrive, responding to the thoughts and questions that I'd sent him late at night. Occasionally, he'd surprise me though: I might write to him at two in the morning and get an answer just half an hour later.

It was an unforgettable period: months for which I shall always be grateful to him and his family. Professor Zygmunt Bauman gave me something priceless, something unique; for him it was just another lesson, one of the many in an extraordinary life.

These are probably the most difficult words I've ever had to write because remembering what I felt on 9 January 2017, while I was staring at the frozen food display in a supermarket, is so painful that it would be worthy of Freudian repression. I had not heard from him for a few days. In the last message he sent, he asked how much I thought he needed to write in order to finish the last chapter of our book. He, the older man, was asking me, the younger one, how much he should write. The greatness of this man was equal only to his humility. Right up to the last days of his life in this world, he lived for his mission: to help people discover the world. Yes, he literally adopted the generations that came after him; he took them by the hand and helped them to really get to know the world and to interpret it.

Zygmunt Bauman had an extraordinary gift: he taught us an analytical method and he lived to build the instruments that allow us to understand where we are and where we're going.

Just before his demise, he wrote to me: 'This book will be on your shoulders, and it must be beautiful and genuine, like you promised me.' When I read that message, I thought he was telling me off for not having yet sent him a finished copy of the full text. I did so straight away. An hour later, he had everything we had written together right up to that day. He never touched on the topic again, and only later, only that day in front of the frozen food cabinet, did I understand what he really meant. He had understood what I couldn't – what I didn't want to – understand. What he had asked for was a symbiotic book: our sixty years' difference – to the day – had to overcome the barrier imposed by modernity and mark out an actual union between discontinuity (me) and continuity (him). This is the point he was stressing.

One of the authors whom Professor Bauman recently liked to quote most often was José Ortega y Gasset, and his theories of 'becoming'. Ortega y Gasset clearly argues that the problem is not the differences between generations. The crucial point is not that generations are different from one another: it is that they all live in the same world at the same time. Above all, he reminds us that generations define themselves in relation to their reciprocal existence. For Hans Jonas, the awareness of being mortal makes passing time important. And we can certainly say that we're the only living beings to have such a manifestly comprehensive awareness. But is having this awareness really such a good thing? Jonas himself has answered the question:

> I am in the prime of my intellectual faculties, I can think, I can be interested in things, read books, read what others say, and talk to them, but as the years pass I understand less and less of modern poetry, contemporary music doesn't please me much; quite simply, I don't accept other experiences. I am already full to the brim, I can't absorb any more. Unlike me, the young people around me aren't burdened by the weight of past experiences.

In short, for Jonas, the passage of time gives authority to habits that have not yet become established. And, by their very nature, the young cannot invent habits that have the weight of time on their side. Therefore, intergenerational relations can be summed up as a problem of continuity and discontinuity. It is precisely this relationship that, according to Professor Bauman, generates the present and will generate the future.

Throughout his extraordinary life, Zygmunt Bauman stressed the fact that we have progress, we have history, thanks to this dialectic between continuity and discontinuity. You cannot talk about the elderly except in opposition to the young; parents/children, teachers/pupils – they are all defined thanks to this interdependent relationship. We all pass, or we have passed, through one or more of these dichotomous definitions.

But in *liquid modernity* everything has changed. Every one of us, living on the stage of the present, is aware of the impotence of the tools we have. We are players on a world stage, but when the spotlights are on us, we are struck by an inability to interpret sensations and perform simple tasks.

If Max Weber's theory of instrumental rationality was the best representation of reality when Bauman was growing up – because there were clear goals to be attained, and it was a question of finding the best means of realizing them – today, at best, those who are *born liquid* only have the means. Yes, they have resources, a handful of skills and talents. But, at a subconscious level, all that any of them can do is to ask themselves constantly: what can I possibly do with all of this?

Zygmunt Bauman knew this well. And he also knew that the proliferation of the generational struggle is merely an illusion.

I think this is what prompted him to choose a person like me to deliver his last lesson. I think this is why he chose to work on this short book with such passion and dedication.

Thomas Leoncini